The Complete Air Fryer Cookbook for Family and Friends

Quick and Delicious Recipes for Every Day incl. Side Dishes, Desserts and More

Martin A. Hammond

TABLE OF CONTENTS

Introduction

What Is An Air Fryer?

An air fryer is a countertop appliance used to make food crispy on the outside and soft on the inside. Unlike a deep fryer, air fryers use little to no oil and hot air to "fry" food. Air fryers allow you to enjoy all your favourite fried foods in a healthier way.

Instead of submerging your food in oil in a deep fryer, you place your food in a tray, basket or bowl inside the air fryer. Air is heated to a set temperature and fans circulate the hot air around the food. The hot air cooks the food quickly for a set time and heats the small amount of oil on the outside of the food, giving it a crispy, fried texture.

Air fryers are very convenient and easy to use. No time is wasted heating up cooking oil. You can prepare and put your ingredients in the air fryer, set the time and temperature, walk away and come back to a tasty fried snack or meal.

Deep-frying food with too much oil adds fat and unnecessary calories to your diet which can lead to serious health issues, such as diabetes and obesity. Using very little oil to no oil in an air fryer significantly reduces the fat content of your meals. Air fried food will taste slightly different from deep-fried food as much less oil is used. Air fried food tastes like extra-crispy oven-baked food and in many cases will taste better. In this book, you will find recipes to help you find creative ways to enjoy fried foods, including meat, fish, and vegetables, to maintain a healthy diet.

Benefits of Using Air Fryers

- Uses little to no oil
- Reduced fat and calories
- Easy to set up and use
- Hands-free cooking
- Safe to use
- Multiple uses
- Easy to clean
- Efficient

What Is The Best Air Fryer To Buy?

Air fryers have recently exploded in popularity and are quickly becoming a household appliance favourite. If you regularly enjoy fried foods an air fryer is worth having. You can find air fryers from all the popular household kitchen appliance brands, varying in price. The cheapest models have the basic functions to manually set the time and temperature and usually have a smaller capacity too. The price of an air fryer increases with size and number of extra features. Premium smart air fryers allow you to control the appliance with an app on your phone. Some air fryers consist of multiple compartments, giving you the extra space to cook large cuts of meat or several meals at once.

All air fryers work in the same way by circulating hot air, similar to a convection oven. There are two main types of air fryers; air fryers with a tray or basket and air fryers with a bowl. The first type of air fryers include a tray or basket, typically located in the back of the device, that you add food to and slot in. The disadvantage with this type of air fryer is it does not allow you to check the progress of your food without pulling out the tray or basket, leading to longer cooking times. Air fryers with a bowl typically have a viewing window in the lid so you can check on the food without interfering with the cooking process.

When buying an air fryer, you may also want to consider whether you would benefit from one which includes a stirring paddle or rotating basket. Having a paddle that automatically stirs your food saves you from having to stir or turn over the food yourself. This ensures your food is cooked evenly although not necessary to successfully cook your meal.

Air fryers are very versatile and can be used to cook a range of meal types, including snacks and desserts. Some air fryers give you the option of grilling your food which can come in handy for recipes that include meat and fish. Be sure to also check if your air fryer is dishwasher safe and wait for the air fryer to cool down before cleaning.

The most popular air fryers are 3 - 5 litres, well suited for families. A 3-litre air fryer is a great option if you don't have much counter space available. If you often entertain large numbers of people, a 6-10 litre air fryer will give you the capacity to cook more food in fewer batches. Review the size guide below to help you decide which size air fryer best suits your needs.

Air Fryer Size Guide

Size	Capacity
1-2 litre	1-2 people
3-5 litre	2-5 people
6-10 litre	6+ people

How Do You Use An Air Fryer?

Using an air fryer couldn't be easier. Once you have prepared your ingredients with little to no oil, add them to the tray, basket or bowl, load the food into the air fryer, set the temperature and time settings, and let the air fryer do the rest. Just like any oven, your air fryer may need a few minutes to preheat. The digital display will show you when the air fryer has reached its set temperature and is ready to use. Assume a 3-litre air fryer is used for the recipes in this book.

Adding oil to the outside of your food will get you the crispy fried texture. Choose a healthy oil like olive oil, coconut oil or avocado oil. Be sure to spray the food whilst out of the air fryer to prevent build up in the appliance and ensure the food is evenly coated. You may want to add an extra layer of oil halfway through the cooking time to get the food extra crispy. Adding a piece of bread under your food is a simple way to soak up any grease.

It's very important you don't overload your air fryer tray, basket or bowl. Giving the food enough space ensures it cooks evenly and thoroughly. To prepare more food try cooking in batches. Many air fryers come with accessories that you can use such as a grill rack, muffin tins, and fine mesh baskets. Whichever you use be sure they fit comfortably in the air fryer compartment. Having a thermometer handy can be useful for checking if your meat has reached the right temperature. To ensure successful preparation of air fried foods, follow the do's and don'ts listed below.

Air Fryer Do's & Don'ts

Do's

- Preheat your air fryer
- Use little to no oil
- Shake basket halfway through cooking time

- Spread food out in a single layer
- Use to reheat food
- Use parchment paper to avoid sticking
- Use a rack to keep lightweight foods down

Don'ts

- Overfill
- Clean whilst still hot
- Scratch non-stick surfaces
- Use higher temperatures to save time

RECIPES

MEAT

SPICY FRIED CHICKEN

> Time: 35 mins | Serves 4
> Net carbs: 1g | Fat: 15g
> Protein: 48g | Kcal: 578

INGREDIENTS

- 500g chicken breast
- 125ml whole milk
- 40g whey protein powder
- 45g grated parmesan
- ¼ tsp salt
- ½ tsp paprika
- 1 tsp ground cayenne pepper
- 2 eggs
- 2 tbsp olive oil

INSTRUCTIONS

1. Preheat your air fryer to 240 degrees Celsius and line the air fryer tray or baking pan with foil.
2. Place the chicken breast and whole milk in a large bowl. Cover and marinate in the fridge overnight.
3. In a shallow bowl, toss the protein powder, parmesan, salt, cayenne pepper and paprika together.
4. Whisk the egg in a separate bowl.
5. Dip the chicken into the egg and then into the protein powder mix. Place the chicken breast on the prepared sheet tray and, once they are all dipped, drizzle with the olive oil.
6. Bake in the air fryer for 15 minutes or until the tenders are golden brown.
7. Serve while hot.

BBQ FRIED CHICKEN

Time: 35 mins | Serves 4
Net carbs: 2g | Fat: 19g
Protein: 48g | Kcal: 540

INGREDIENTS

- 500g chicken breast
- 125ml whole milk
- 40g whey protein powder
- 45g grated parmesan
- ¼ tsp salt
- ¼ tsp ground black pepper
- ½ tsp paprika
- 2 eggs
- 2 tbsp olive oil
- 300g keto BBQ sauce

INSTRUCTIONS

1 Preheat your air fryer to 240 degrees Celsius and line the air fryer tray or baking pan with foil.
2 Place the chicken breast and whole milk in a large bowl. Cover and marinate in the fridge overnight.
3 In a shallow bowl, toss the protein powder, parmesan, salt, pepper and paprika together.
4 Whisk the egg in a separate bowl.
5 Dip the chicken into the egg and then into the protein powder mix. Place the chicken breast on the prepared sheet tray and, once they are all dipped, drizzle with the olive oil.
6 Bake in the air fryer for 15 minutes or until the tenders are golden brown.
7 Serve with the BBQ sauce on the side for dipping and serve while hot.

BUFFALO CHICKEN PIZZA

> Time: 40 mins | Serves 3
> Net carbs: 10g | Fat: 26g
> Protein: 25g | Kcal: 389

INGREDIENTS

- 125g almond flour
- 1 egg
- 3 tbsp water
- 4 tbsp fresh grated parmesan
- 1 tbsp fresh chopped basil
- 115g fresh diced mozzarella
- 140g shredded cooked chicken
- 1/3 cup keto buffalo sauce

INSTRUCTIONS

1. Preheat your air fryer to 190 degrees Celsius and line the air fryer tray or baking pan with foil.
2. In a medium-sized bowl, mix the almond flour and water.
3. Add the egg and parmesan to the bowl and knead into a soft dough.
4. Place the dough on the prepared tray and press into a flat circle, about 0.5 cm thick.
5. In a separate bowl, toss the shredded chicken with the buffalo sauce.
6. Spread the chicken mix over the dough and then top with the fresh basil and mozzarella.
7. Place in the preheated air fryer and bake for 18 minutes or until the cheese is melted and bubbling.
8. Slice and serve.

CHICKEN NUGGETS

Time: 25 mins | Serves 4
Net carbs: 0g | Fat: 18g
Protein: 24g | Kcal: 278

INGREDIENTS

- 500g chicken breast
- 60g mayonnaise
- 2 tbsp mustard
- ½ tsp salt
- ½ tsp ground black pepper
- 40g ground pork skin
- 2 tbsp whole milk

INSTRUCTIONS

1 Preheat your air fryer to 200 degrees Celsius and line your air fryer tray with foil and spray with cooking oil.
2 Dry the chicken breast by patting with a paper towel. Cut the chicken into strips about 2.5 cm wide and 5 cm long.
3 In a small bowl, combine the mustard, mayo and milk and stir together well.
4 In a separate bowl, combine the ground pork skin, salt and pepper.
5 Dip the chicken nuggets into the mayonnaise mix and then into the pork rind mix, coating the chicken completely.
6 Place it on the prepared tray when done and repeat with the remaining chicken pieces.
7 Place the tray in the air fryer and bake the chicken for 8 minutes, flip and bake for another 7 minutes.
8 Serve while hot.

ROTISSERIE-STYLE CHICKEN THIGHS

> Time: 50 mins | Serves 4
> Net carbs: 0g | Fat: 13g
> Protein: 24g | Kcal: 199

INGREDIENTS

- 3 tbsp olive oil
- 500g chicken thighs
- ½ tsp sea salt
- ¼ tsp ground black pepper

INSTRUCTIONS

1. Preheat your air fryer to 200 degrees Celsius and prepare your air fryer tray with a piece of foil.
2. In a large bowl, whisk together 2 tbsp of the olive oil, salt and pepper.
3. Add the chicken to the bowl and toss to coat. Cover the bowl and place in the fridge for two hours.
4. Add the remaining tablespoon of olive oil to a sauté pan and heat over high. Sear the marinated chicken on each side for 3 minutes, just to brown.
5. Move the browned chicken to the prepared, foil-lined tray and pour the remaining marinade from the bowl over the chicken.
6. Place the tray in the preheated air fryer for 20 minutes until the skin is crispy.
7. Serve hot.

LEMON GARLIC CHICKEN THIGHS

Time: 50 mins | Serves 4
Net carbs: 1g | Fat: 14g
Protein: 24g | Kcal: 201

INGREDIENTS

- 3 tbsp olive oil
- 3 tbsp lemon juice
- 3 tbsp minced garlic
- 500g chicken thighs
- ½ tsp sea salt
- ¼ tsp ground black pepper
- 1 lemon, sliced thinly

INSTRUCTIONS

1. Preheat your air fryer to 200 degrees Celsius and prepare your air fryer tray with a piece of foil.
2. In a large bowl, whisk together 2 tbsp of the olive oil, lemon juice, and garlic.
3. Add the chicken to the bowl and toss to coat. Cover the bowl and place in the fridge for two hours.
4. Add the remaining tablespoon of olive oil to a sauté pan and heat over high. Sear the marinated chicken on each side for 3 minutes, just to brown.
5. Move the browned chicken to the prepared, foil-lined tray and pour the remaining marinade from the bowl over the chicken.
6. Add the lemon slices, layering them over and around the chicken.
7. Place the tray in the preheated air fryer for 20 minutes.
8. Serve hot.

TERIYAKI CHICKEN MELT CUPS

Time: 30 mins | Serves 7
Net carbs: 4g | Fat: 14g
Protein: 12g | Kcal: 201

INGREDIENTS

- 300g shredded cooked chicken
- 2 eggs
- 60g sour cream
- 60g mayonnaise
- 2 tbsp keto teriyaki sauce
- 180g shredded cheddar cheese
- ¼ tsp salt
- ¼ tsp ground black pepper
- 1 tbsp parsley, chopped

INSTRUCTIONS

1 Preheat your air fryer to 160 degrees Celsius and grease a muffin tin or individual muffin cups.
2 In a large bowl, combine the chicken, mayonnaise, sour cream, grated cheese, parsley, teriyaki sauce, salt and pepper.
3 Scoop the mix into the prepared muffin tin, filling each cup to the top.
4 Bake in the air fryer for 20 minutes or until the tops are golden brown.
5 Serve on a slice of bread, crackers or plain with a spoon.

CHICKEN PATTIES

Time: 1 ½ hours | Serves 8
Net carbs: 1g | Fat: 27g
Protein: 30g | Kcal: 343

INGREDIENTS

- 400g shredded, cooked chicken
- 100g pork skin, crushed
- 225g mozzarella cheese, grated
- 1 tbsp keto mayonnaise
- 2 eggs
- ½ tsp smoked paprika
- 3 tbsp water
- 2 tbsp olive oil

INSTRUCTIONS

1 Preheat your air fryer to 190 degrees Celsius and line your air fryer tray with foil or parchment.

2 Place all the ingredients except for the olive oil, in a large bowl and blend well using your hands.

3 Cover the bowl and refrigerate for an hour to let the flavours soak together.

4 Remove the bowl from the fridge and use your hands to form the tuna cakes, making each patty about 2.5 cm thick.

5 Place the cakes on the prepared sheet tray and drizzle with olive oil.

6 Cook the cakes in the air fryer for about 7 minutes or until golden brown.

7 Remove from the air fryer and serve while hot.

PROSCIUTTO WRAPPED CHICKEN

> Time: 20 mins | Serves 2
> Net carbs: 9g | Fat: 17g
> Protein: 41g | Kcal: 582

INGREDIENTS

- 500g chicken breast
- ¼ tsp salt
- ¼ tsp ground black pepper
- 50g prosciutto de parma, very thinly sliced
- 2 tbsp olive oil
- 1 tsp minced garlic
- 120g baby spinach
- 2 tsp lemon juice

INSTRUCTIONS

1. Preheat your air fryer to 160 degrees Celsius and line your air fryer tray with foil.
2. Dry the chicken by patting with a paper towel then cut into strips and sprinkle with salt and pepper.
3. Wrap the chicken breast in the prosciutto.
4. Place the wrapped chicken breast on the prepared tray.
5. Toss the spinach with the olive oil, garlic and lemon juice and place on the tray as well, around the wrapped chicken.
6. Place in the air fryer and bake for 12 minutes.
7. Serve while hot.

FAJITA CHICKEN

Time: 40 mins | Serves 5
Net carbs: 3g | Fat: 11g
Protein: 37g | Kcal: 272

INGREDIENTS

- 875g chicken breast, cut thinly into strips
- 2 tsp fajita seasoning
- 75g sliced green bell peppers
- 4 tbsp olive oil

INSTRUCTIONS

1 Preheat your air fryer to 200 degrees Celsius and line your air fryer tray with a long piece of parchment paper.

2 Place the chicken breast on the parchment and sprinkle with the fajita seasoning and rub the spices into the chicken.

3 Add the remaining ingredients and then wrap the parchment paper up around the chicken breast, enclosing them completely.

4 Place the tray in the air fryer and bake for 20 minutes.

5 Remove from the air fryer, unwrap the parchment and serve while hot.

CLASSIC MEATBALLS

Time: 35 mins | Serves 4
Net carbs: 5g | Fat: 4g
Protein: 33g | Kcal: 201

INGREDIENTS

- 500g minced beef
- 170g mozzarella cheese, shredded
- 25g fresh grated parmesan
- 1 tsp Italian seasoning
- ¼ tsp ground black pepper
- ¼ tsp salt
- 1 tbsp almond flour

INSTRUCTIONS

1. Preheat your air fryer to 180 degrees Celsius and line the air fryer tray with a piece of foil.
2. In a large mixing bowl, combine the beef, cheeses, Italian seasoning, pepper, salt and almond flour. Blend well.
3. Roll the meat mixture into evenly sized balls and place on the prepared tray.
4. Bake for 25 minutes.
5. Serve the meatballs while hot.

CHEESY ITALIAN MEATLOAF

> Time: 50 mins | Serves 4
> Net carbs: 5g | Fat: 5g
> Protein: 33g | Kcal: 279

INGREDIENTS

- 500g minced beef
- 170g mozzarella cheese, shredded
- 25g fresh grated parmesan
- 1 tsp Italian seasoning
- ¼ tsp ground black pepper
- ¼ tsp salt
- 1 tbsp almond flour
- 1 tbsp tomato paste
- 1 tbsp monk fruit sweetener
- 1 tsp apple cider vinegar
- 1 tsp Dijon mustard

INSTRUCTIONS

1. Preheat your air fryer to 180 degrees Celsius and grease a loaf pan that will fit in the air fryer basket.
2. In a large mixing bowl, combine the beef, cheeses, Italian seasoning, pepper, salt and almond flour. Blend well and then place in a greased loaf pan.
3. Bake for 35 minutes.
4. While the meatloaf is baking, combine the tomato paste, monk fruit sweetener, vinegar and mustard. Mix well.
5. Once the meatloaf is done, spoon the sauce over the top and then slice and serve.

ITALIAN LASAGNA

Time: 20 mins | Serves 2
Net carbs: 6g | Fat: 31g
Protein: 29g | Kcal: 389

INGREDIENTS

- ½ large zucchini, sliced thinly
- 240g crumbled, cooked minced beef
- 3 tbsp marinara sauce
- 2 tbsp ricotta, whole milk
- 1 tsp Italian seasoning
- 55g fresh chopped mozzarella

INSTRUCTIONS

1 Preheat your air fryer to 200 degrees Celsius.
2 Mix the ricotta and Italian seasoning.
3 Get an oven-safe large ramekin or mug.
4 Lay some of the zucchini slices in the bottom of the cup.
5 Spread about 1 tablespoon of the ricotta on top of the zucchini then top with a tablespoon of the marinara sauce.
6 Top with foil-lined minced beef.
7 Layer more zucchini on top of the marinara and repeat the layering process until you have used all the zucchini, ricotta, minced beef and marinara.
8 Top with the mozzarella.
9 Place the lasagna in the oven and bake for 15 minutes or until the mozzarella is melted and bubbly.
10 Serve while hot.

CREAMY GARLIC PORK CHOPS

Time: 50 mins | Serves 4
Net carbs: 6g | Fat: 18g
Protein: 27g | Kcal: 278

INGREDIENTS

- 3 tbsp olive oil
- 3 tbsp lemon juice
- 3 tbsp minced garlic
- 1 tsp oregano, dried
- 500g pork chops
- ½ tsp sea salt
- ¼ tsp ground black pepper
- 250g asparagus
- 1 zucchini, sliced thinly
- 1 lemon, sliced thinly
- 120g heavy cream

INSTRUCTIONS

1. Preheat your air fryer to 200 degrees Celsius and prepare your air fryer tray with a piece of foil.
2. In a large bowl, whisk together 2 tbsp of the olive oil, lemon juice, dried oregano and garlic.
3. Add the pork chops to the bowl and toss to coat. Cover the bowl and place in the fridge for two hours.
4. Add the remaining tablespoon of olive oil to a saute pan and heat over high. Sear the marinated pork chops on each side for 3 minutes, just to brown.
5. Move the browned pork chops to the prepared, foil lined tray and pour the remaining marinade from the bowl over the chops.
6. Add the asparagus, zucchini and lemon slices, layering them over and around the pork chops.

7   Place the tray in the preheated air fryer for 20 minutes. Remove the tray from the fryer and whisk in the heavy cream.
8   Return to the air fryer for another 5 minutes then serve hot.

MINTY LAMB CHOPS

Time: 50 mins | Serves 4
Net carbs: 5g | Fat: 8g
Protein: 25g | Kcal: 263

INGREDIENTS

- 3 tbsp olive oil
- 3 tbsp lemon juice
- 1 tbsp fresh chopped mint
- 500g lamb chops
- ½ tsp sea salt
- ¼ tsp ground black pepper
- 1 zucchini, sliced thinly
- 90g baby spinach

INSTRUCTIONS

1 Preheat your air fryer to 200 degrees Celsius and prepare your air fryer tray with a piece of foil.
2 In a large bowl, whisk together 2 tbsp of the olive oil, lemon juice, and mint.
3 Add the lamb chops to the bowl and toss to coat. Cover the bowl and place in the fridge for two hours.
4 Add the remaining tablespoon of olive oil to a saute pan and heat over high. Sear the marinated lamb chops on each side for 3 minutes, just to brown.
5 Move the browned pork lamb to the prepared, foil-lined tray and pour the remaining marinade from the bowl over the chops.
6 Add the zucchini and baby spinach, placing them over and around the lamb chops.
7 Place the tray in the preheated air fryer for 20 minutes.
8 Serve while hot.

FISH

SALMON AND ASPARAGUS

Time: 40 mins | Serves 5
Net carbs: 6g | Fat: 10g
Protein: 33g | Kcal: 257

INGREDIENTS

- 880g salmon fillets
- ¼ tsp salt
- ¼ tsp ground black pepper
- 3 tbsp olive oil
- 500g asparagus spears
- 1 tbsp lemon juice
- 1 tbsp fresh chopped parsley

INSTRUCTIONS

1. Preheat your air fryer to 200 degrees Celsius and line your air fryer tray with a long piece of parchment paper.
2. Place the salmon fillets on the parchment, sprinkle with the salt and pepper and rub the spices into the fish.
3. Top the fish with the remaining ingredients and then wrap the parchment paper up around the fish filets, enclosing them completely.
4. Place the tray in the air fryer and bake for 20 minutes.
5. Remove from the air fryer, unwrap the parchment and serve while hot.

DIJON BAKED SALMON

Time: 25 mins | Serves 5
Net carbs: 1g | Fat: 13g
Protein: 31g | Kcal: 250

INGREDIENTS

- 750g salmon
- 8g parsley, freshly chopped
- 75g Dijon mustard
- 1 tbsp olive oil
- 1 tbsp freshly squeezed lemon juice
- 1 tbsp minced garlic
- ¼ tsp salt
- ¼ tsp ground black pepper

INSTRUCTIONS

1 Preheat your air fryer to 190 degrees Celsius and line your air fryer tray with a piece of parchment paper.
2 Place the salmon on the parchment-lined tray.
3 In a small bowl, mix the remaining ingredients and then spread over the top of the salmon.
4 Place the salmon in the air fryer and bake for 18 minutes.
5 Slice and serve hot.

RED HOT TUNA CAKES

Time: 1 ½ hours | Serves 8
Net carbs: 1g | Fat: 25g
Protein: 23g | Kcal: 318

INGREDIENTS

- 280g canned, drained tuna
- 115g pork skin, crushed
- 225g mozzarella cheese, grated
- 1 tbsp keto mayonnaise
- 2 eggs
- ½ tsp smoked paprika
- 1 tsp red pepper flakes
- 3 tbsp water
- 2 tbsp olive oil

INSTRUCTIONS

1 Preheat your air fryer to 190 degrees Celsius and line your air fryer tray with foil or parchment.

2 Place all the ingredients in a large bowl, except for the olive oil, and blend well using your hands.

3 Cover the bowl and refrigerate for an hour.

4 Remove the bowl from the fridge and use your hands to form the tuna cakes, making each patty about 2.5 cm thick.

5 Place the cakes on the prepared sheet tray and drizzle with olive oil.

6 Cook the cakes in the air fryer for about 7 minutes or until golden brown.

7 Remove from the air fryer and serve while hot.

TUNA STICKS

> Time: 20 mins | Serves 4
> Net carbs: 0g | Fat: 18g
> Protein: 27g | Kcal: 274

INGREDIENTS

- 500g tuna
- 60g mayonnaise
- 2 tbsp mustard
- ½ tsp salt
- ½ tsp ground black pepper
- 45g ground pork skin
- 2 tbsp whole milk

INSTRUCTIONS

1. Preheat your air fryer to 200 degrees Celsius and line your air fryer tray with foil and spray with cooking oil.
2. Dry the tuna filets by patting with a paper towel.
3. Cut the fish into strips about 2.5 cm wide and 5 cm long.
4. In a small bowl, combine the mustard, mayo and milk and stir together well.
5. In a separate bowl, combine the ground pork skin, salt and pepper.
6. Dip the fish strips into the mayonnaise mix and then into the pork rind mix, coating the fish completely.
7. Place it on the prepared tray when done and repeat with the remaining fish sticks.
8. Place the tray in the air fryer and bake the fish for 5 minutes, flip and bake for another 5 minutes.
9. Serve while hot.

GARLIC SHRIMP TUNA BAKE

Time: 20 mins | Serves 4
Net carbs: 3g | Fat: 30g
Protein: 43g | Kcal: 376

INGREDIENTS

- 230g butter
- 2 tbsp minced garlic
- 500g shrimp, peeled and cleaned
- ¼ tsp ground black pepper
- 25g canned tuna, drained well
- 80g heavy cream
- 25g parmesan cheese

INSTRUCTIONS

1 Preheat your air fryer to 200 degrees Celsius and grease an 8x8 inch (20x20 cm) baking pan.
2 Add the butter and shrimp to the pan and place in the air fryer for 3 minutes.
3 Remove the pan from the air fryer.
4 Add the remaining ingredients to the pan and return to the air fryer to cook for another 5 minutes. The mix should be bubbling and the shrimp should be pink.
5 Serve while hot.

LEMON PEPPER FISH STICKS

Time: 20 mins | Serves 4
Net carbs: 0g | Fat: 16g
Protein: 26g | Kcal: 265

INGREDIENTS

- 500g cod
- 60g mayonnaise
- 2 tbsp mustard
- ½ tsp salt
- 1 tsp lemon pepper seasoning
- 45g ground pork skin
- 2 tbsp whole milk

INSTRUCTIONS

1. Preheat your air fryer to 200 degrees Celcius and line your air fryer tray with foil and spray with cooking oil.
2. Dry the cod filets by patting with a paper towel.
3. Cut the fish into strips about 2.5 cm wide and 5 cm long.
4. In a small bowl, combine the mustard, mayo and milk and stir together well.
5. In a separate bowl, combine the ground pork skin, lemon pepper and salt.
6. Dip the fish strips into the mayonnaise mix and then into the pork rind mix, coating the fish completely. Place it on the prepared tray when done and repeat with the remaining fish sticks.
7. Place the tray in the air fryer and bake the fish for 5 minutes, flip and bake for another 5 minutes.
8. Serve while hot.

LEMON DILL WRAPPED COD

> Time: 20 mins | Serves 2
> Net carbs: 9g | Fat: 20g
> Protein: 49g | Kcal: 430

INGREDIENTS

- 500g cod fillets
- ¼ tsp salt
- ¼ tsp ground black pepper
- 1 tsp lemon zest
- 1 tbsp chopped fresh dill
- 55g prosciutto de parma, very thinly sliced
- 2 tbsp olive oil
- 1 tsp minced garlic
- 120g baby spinach
- 2 tsp lemon juice

INSTRUCTIONS

1 Preheat your air fryer to 160 degrees Celsius and line your air fryer tray with foil.
2 Dry the cod fillets by patting with a paper towel then sprinkle with salt and pepper.
3 Sprinkle the lemon zest and dill on the filets as well.
4 Wrap the filets in the prosciutto, enclosing them as fully as possible.
5 Place the wrapped fillets on the prepared tray.
6 Toss the spinach with the olive oil, garlic and lemon juice and place on the tray as well, around the wrapped cod.
7 Place in the air fryer and bake for 12 minutes.
8 Serve hot!

CREAMY BAKED SCALLOPS

Time: 10 mins | Serves 4
Net carbs: 2g | Fat: 10g
Protein: 13g | Kcal: 174

INGREDIENTS

- 500g jumbo scallops
- 1 tbsp butter
- 1 tbsp heavy cream
- ¼ tsp salt
- ¼ tsp ground black pepper

INSTRUCTIONS

1. Preheat your air fryer to 200 degrees Celsius and line your air fryer tray with foil.
2. Place the butter on the air fryer tray and place inside the air fryer for one minute to melt.
3. Remove the tray and add the scallops, heavy cream, and seasonings, toss together and return to the air fryer for 5 minutes. The bottom of the scallops should be golden brown.
4. Serve while hot.

CRAB STUFFED MUSHROOMS

Time: 1 ½ hours | Serves 5
Net carbs: 6g | Fat: 18g
Protein: 24g | Kcal: 211

INGREDIENTS

- 500g mushrooms, stems and gills removed
- 340g fresh crab meat
- 170g cheese, softened
- 80g grated cheddar cheese
- 60g sour cream
- 1 tbsp minced garlic
- 1 tbsp mustard
- ½ tsp salt
- ¼ tsp ground black pepper
- 45g grated parmesan

INSTRUCTIONS

1 Preheat your air fryer to 190 degrees Celsius and line your air fryer tray with foil or parchment.
2 Place the mushroom caps on the tray and bake for 10 minutes in the air fryer.
3 Remove the tray from the air fryer and drain any excess water.
4 In a large mixing bowl, combine all the remaining ingredients except the parmesan cheese. Stir well to fully blend everything.
5 Stuff the mushroom caps with the crab mix and then sprinkle the parmesan over the top of the mushrooms.
6 Return the tray to the air fryer and bake for another 10 minutes or until the tops of the mushrooms are golden brown.
7 Remove from the air fryer and serve while hot.

GARLIC BUTTER SHRIMP

Time: 15 mins | Serves 4
Net carbs: 3g | Fat: 20g
Protein: 27g | Kcal: 307

INGREDIENTS

- 500g shrimp, cleaned completely
- 5 tbsp butter, melted
- ½ tsp ground black pepper
- ½ tsp salt
- 125ml vegetable stock
- 2 tbsp lemon juice
- 60g minced garlic
- 2 tbsp parsley

INSTRUCTIONS

1. Preheat your air fryer to 180 degrees Celsius and line the air fryer tray or baking pan with foil.
2. Place the shrimp, butter, pepper, salt, vegetable stock, and garlic in a large bowl and toss together well.
3. Pour the mix onto the prepared tray or pan.
4. Bake for 12 minutes, stirring occasionally to flip the shrimp.
5. Divide onto plates and garnish with lemon juice and garlic.
6. Serve while hot.

VEGGIE

SPICY EGG SALAD

> Time: 20 mins | Serves 6
> Net carbs: 1g | Fat: 12g
> Protein: 12g | Kcal: 189

INGREDIENTS

- 6 tbsp Mayonnaise
- 8 Large Eggs
- 2 tbsp apple cider vinegar
- 1 tsp ground black pepper
- 1 tsp salt
- ¼ tsp paprika
- 1 tsp cayenne pepper, ground

INSTRUCTIONS

1. Preheat your air fryer to 120 degrees Celsius.
2. Place a wire rack in the air fryer and place the eggs on top of the rack.
3. Cook for 16 minutes then remove the eggs and place them directly into an ice water bath to cool and stop the cooking process.
4. Peel the eggs and place in a large bowl.
5. Mash the eggs with a fork.
6. Add in the mayonnaise, cider vinegar, pepper, cayenne, paprika and salt.

ROASTED VEGGIE SOUP

Time: 35 mins | Serves 4
Net carbs: 2g | Fat: 8g
Protein: 4g | Kcal: 209

INGREDIENTS

- 180g chopped cauliflower
- 140g chopped broccoli
- 150g green bell pepper
- 115g chopped carrot
- 3 tbsp olive oil
- 1 tsp sea salt

- ¼ tsp ground black pepper
- 2 tbsp minced garlic
- 25g diced onion
- 1 tbsp dried chopped thyme
- 1 L vegetable broth
- 240g heavy cream

INSTRUCTIONS

1 Preheat your air fryer to 200 degrees Celsius and line the air fryer tray or baking pan with foil.

2 Place the cauliflower, broccoli, bell pepper, carrots, garlic and onion on the prepared sheet tray.

3 Sprinkle the veggies with the salt, black pepper, thyme and olive oil.

4 Roast in the air fryer for 20 minutes or until the cauliflower is tender.

5 Add the roasted veggies to a blender or food processor and add the veggie broth and heavy cream.

6 Puree until smooth.

7 Serve while hot.

PUMPKIN SOUP

Time: 35 mins | Serves 4
Net carbs: 9g | Fat: 22g
Protein: 5g | Kcal: 215

INGREDIENTS

- 480g chopped fresh pumpkin
- 3 tbsp olive oil
- 1 tsp sea salt
- ¼ tsp ground black pepper
- 180g chopped carrots
- 15g diced onion
- 1 tbsp dried chopped thyme
- 1L chicken broth
- 240g heavy cream

INSTRUCTIONS

1. Preheat your air fryer to 200 degrees Celsius and line the air fryer tray or baking pan with foil.
2. Place the pumpkin, carrots, and onion on the prepared sheet tray.
3. Sprinkle the veggies with salt, black pepper, thyme and olive oil.
4. Roast in the air fryer for 20 minutes or until the squash is tender.
5. Add the roasted veggies to a blender or food processor and add the chicken broth and heavy cream.
6. Puree until smooth.
7. Serve while hot.

SPINACH AND SUNDRIED TOMATO CASSEROLE

Time: 40 mins | Serves 12
Net carbs: 7g | Fat: 16g
Protein: 16g | Kcal: 247

INGREDIENTS

- 16 eggs
- 50ml whole milk
- 115g chopped sundried tomatoes
- 250g frozen, chopped spinach, thawed, drained
- 235g cheddar cheese, grated
- 45g grated parmesan cheese
- 125g whole milk ricotta
- 8g chopped white onion
- 1 tsp minced garlic
- 1 tsp sea salt
- ½ tsp dried thyme
- ½ tsp ground black pepper

INSTRUCTIONS

1 Preheat your air fryer to 180 degrees Celsius and prepare a large baking dish with baking oil.
2 Whisk the eggs and milk in a large bowl.
3 Add the sundried tomatoes and spinach to the egg mix.
4 Add all the remaining ingredients, except the ricotta, and stir well.
5 Pour the egg and veggie mix into the prepared tray.
6 Dollop the ricotta around the pan, dispersing it evenly.
7 Bake in the air fryer for 30 minutes or until the eggs are completely set, then serve.

PEPPER STUFFED MUSHROOMS

> <u>Time: 1 hour | Serves 5</u>
> <u>Net carbs: 5g | Fat: 10g</u>
> <u>Protein: 11g | Kcal: 276</u>

INGREDIENTS

- 500g cremini mushrooms, stems and gills removed
- 80g minced bell pepper
- 170g cheese, softened
- 60g grated cheddar cheese
- 60g sour cream
- 2 tbsp minced garlic
- 1 tbsp mustard
- ½ tsp salt
- ¼ tsp ground black pepper
- 45g grated parmesan

INSTRUCTIONS

1. Preheat your air fryer to 190 degrees Celsius and line your air fryer tray with foil or parchment.
2. Place the mushroom caps on the tray and bake for 10 minutes in the air fryer. Remove from the air fryer and drain any excess water from the tray.
3. In a large mixing bowl, combine all the remaining ingredients except the parmesan cheese and stir well.
4. Stuff the mushroom caps with the crab mix and then sprinkle the parmesan over the top of the mushrooms.
5. Return the tray to the air fryer and bake for another 10 minutes or until the tops of the mushrooms are golden brown.
6. Remove from the air fryer and serve while hot.

LOADED VEGGIE PIZZA

Time: 40 mins | Serves 3
Net carbs: 5g | Fat: 10g
Protein: 13g | Kcal: 372

INGREDIENTS

- 125g almond flour
- 1 egg
- 3 tbsp water
- 4 tbsp fresh grated parmesan
- 1 tbsp fresh chopped basil
- 115g fresh diced mozzarella
- 15g chopped tomatoes
- 60g sliced mushrooms
- 55g keto tomato sauce

INSTRUCTIONS

1 Preheat your air fryer to 190 degrees Celsius and line the air fryer tray or baking pan with foil.

2 In a medium sized bowl, mix together the almond flour and water.

3 Add the egg and parmesan to the bowl and knead into a soft dough.

4 Place the dough on the prepared tray and press into a flat circle, about 0.5 cm thick.

5 Spread the tomato sauce over the dough and then top with the fresh basil, tomatoes, mushrooms and mozzarella.

6 Place in the preheated air fryer and bake for 18 minutes or until the cheese is melted and bubbling.

7 Slice and serve.

CARROT CHEESE FRITTERS

> Time: 40 mins | Serves 4
> Net carbs: 7g | Fat: 19g
> Protein: 15g | Kcal: 289

INGREDIENTS

- 95g almond flour
- 7 tbsp ground flaxseeds
- 195g chopped carrots
- 100g grated mozzarella cheese
- 2 eggs
- 2 tsp baking powder
- 1 tsp salt
- ¼ tsp ground black pepper
- 1 tbsp olive oil

INSTRUCTIONS

1 Preheat your air fryer to 200 degrees Celsius and prepare a large baking dish with foil.
2 Place the carrots in a food processor along with the mozzarella, almond flour, 4 tablespoons of the flaxseeds and baking powder. Pulse until the mixture reaches a crumbly texture.
3 Add the eggs, salt and pepper and pulse until a dough forms.
4 Scoop the mix into bite sized balls, rolling them between your hands.
5 Roll the balls in the remaining flaxseeds and place on the prepared baking tray.
6 Drizzle with the olive oil and roll the balls around on the tray so the olive oil is coating the outside.

7   Place in the preheated air fryer and bake for 10 minutes or until nicely golden brown.

8   Serve while hot.

VEGGIE BAKED ZUCCHINI BOATS

Time: 40 mins | Serves 6
Net carbs: 4g | Fat: 8g
Protein: 6g | Kcal: 158

INGREDIENTS

- 3 zucchini, sliced in half, seeds scooped out
- 1 tsp salt
- ½ tsp ground black pepper
- 1 tsp olive oil
- 2 tsp smoked paprika
- 1 cup chopped mushrooms
- 1 cup baby spinach
- 1 cup shredded cheddar cheese
- 3 tbsp sour cream
- 2 tbsp chopped chives

INSTRUCTIONS

1 Preheat your air fryer to 190 degrees Celsius and line the air fryer tray or baking pan with foil.
2 Place the zucchini skins on the prepared tray and sprinkle with the salt.
3 Let sit for 30 minutes then pat the skins dry to remove the water which the salt has extracted.
4 Spread the mushrooms and baby spinach inside the zucchini boats, dividing the filling evenly.
5 Sprinkle the zucchini with the black pepper, paprika and olive oil.
6 Bake for 10 minutes to soften.

7. Remove from the air fryer and top with the cheese. Return to the air fryer for another 10 minutes or until the cheese is bubbly.
8. Remove from the air fryer and top with the sour cream and chives.
9. Serve while hot.

BRUNCH

THREE CHEESE OMELET

Time: 15 mins | Serves 4
Net carbs: 2g | Fat: 16g
Protein: 7g | Kcal: 189

INGREDIENTS

- 4 eggs
- 3 tbsp heavy whipping cream
- 55g cheddar cheese, grated
- 55g feta cheese
- 55g mozzarella cheese
- ½ tsp salt
- ¼ tsp ground black pepper

INSTRUCTIONS

1. Preheat your air fryer to 180 degrees Celsius and line a 7 inch (18 cm) round baking pan with parchment paper.
2. In a small bowl, whisk together the eggs, cream, salt and pepper.
3. Pour the mix into the prepared baking pan and then place the pan in your preheated air fryer.
4. Cook for about 10 minutes or until the eggs are completely set.
5. Sprinkle the cheeses across the cooked eggs and return the pan to the air fryer for another minute to melt the cheese.
6. Fold the omelet in half.
7. Slice into wedges and serve while hot.

VEGGIE OMELET

Time: 25 mins | Serves 2
Net carbs: 1g | Fat: 14g
Protein: 10g | Kcal: 153

INGREDIENTS

- 4 eggs
- 3 tbsp heavy whipping cream
- 115g cheddar cheese, grated
- 30g sliced mushrooms
- 15g baby spinach
- 55g diced tomato
- ½ tsp salt
- ¼ tsp ground black pepper

INSTRUCTIONS

1. Preheat your air fryer to 180 degrees Celsius and line a 7 inch (18 cm) round baking pan with parchment paper.
2. In a small bowl, whisk together the eggs, cream, salt and pepper.
3. Stir the mushrooms, spinach and tomato into the bowl.
4. Pour the mix into the prepared baking pan and then place the pan in your preheated air fryer.
5. Cook for about 15 minutes or until the eggs are completely set.
6. Sprinkle the cheese over half of the omelet then fold the omelet in half, over the cheese.
7. Let sit for 5 minutes to allow the cheese time to melt.
8. Slice into wedges and serve while hot.

BACON AND CHEESE FRITTATA

> Time: 20 mins | Serves 2
> Net carbs: 1g | Fat: 19g
> Protein: 10g | Kcal: 284

INGREDIENTS

- 4 eggs
- 3 tbsp heavy whipping cream
- 115g chopped, cooked bacon
- 115g cheddar cheese, grated
- ½ tsp salt
- ¼ tsp ground black pepper

INSTRUCTIONS

1 Preheat your air fryer to 180 degrees Celsius and line a 7 inch (18 cm) round baking pan with parchment paper.

2 In a small bowl, whisk together the eggs, cream, salt and pepper.

3 Stir the bacon and cheese into the bowl.

4 Pour the mix into the prepared baking pan and then place the pan in your preheated air fryer.

5 Cook for about 15 minutes or until the eggs are completely set.

6 Slice into wedges and serve while hot.

SPINACH PARMESAN BAKED EGGS

Time: 15 mins | Serves 1
Net carbs: 3g | Fat: 11g
Protein: 14g | Kcal: 284

INGREDIENTS

- 2 eggs
- 1 tbsp heavy cream
- 1 tbsp frozen, chopped spinach, thawed
- 1 tbsp grated parmesan cheese
- ¼ tsp salt
- 1/8 tsp ground black pepper

INSTRUCTIONS

1. Preheat your air fryer to 160 degrees Celsius.
2. Spray a silicone muffin cup with cooking spray.
3. In a small bowl, whisk together all the ingredients.
4. Pour the eggs into the prepared ramekin and bake for 7 minutes.
5. Serve straight out of the baking cup.

VEGGIE EGG BREAD

Time: 1 hour | Serves 12
Net carbs: 8g | Fat: 16g
Protein: 6g | Kcal: 215

INGREDIENTS

- 115g chopped tomatoes
- 60g sliced mushrooms, cooked
- 60g almond flour
- 2 tsp baking powder
- ½ tsp ground black pepper
- 1 tsp salt
- 250g cream cheese
- 10 eggs
- 120g grated zucchini
- 235g grated cheddar cheese

INSTRUCTIONS

1. Preheat your air fryer to 180 degrees Celsius and line a 7 inch (18 cm) round baking pan with parchment paper.
2. Whisk together the almond flour, salt, pepper and baking powder.
3. In a separate bowl, beat the cream cheese until it is nice and smooth then add the eggs.
4. Beat until well combined.
5. Add the zucchini to the cream cheese mix and stir until incorporated.
6. Add the dry mixture to the cream cheese bowl and stir well.
7. Fold in the cheddar cheese, tomatoes and cooked mushrooms.
8. Pour into the prepared pan and cook in the air fryer for 45 minutes.
9. Let cool slightly before slicing and serving.

COCONUT CHOCOLATE PANCAKE

Time: 20 mins | Serves 2
Net carbs: 4g | Fat: 14g
Protein: 9g | Kcal: 223

INGREDIENTS

- 2 eggs
- 125ml whole milk
- 2 tbsp butter, melted
- 1 tsp vanilla extract
- 150g coconut flour
- 2 tbsp cocoa powder
- 3 tbsp granulated sweetener
- 1 tsp baking powder
- 1/8 tsp salt
- 90g shredded, unsweetened coconut

INSTRUCTIONS

1 Preheat your air fryer to 200 degrees Celsius and line a 7 inch (18 cm) round baking pan with parchment paper.
2 Place the eggs, milk, butter and vanilla extract in a blender and puree for about thirty seconds.
3 Add the remaining ingredients to the blender and puree until smooth.
4 Pour the pancake batter into the prepared pan and stir in the shredded coconut.
5 Place in the air fryer.
6 Cook for 9 minutes or until the pancake is puffed and the top is golden brown.
7 Slice and serve.

RASPBERRY ALMOND PANCAKE

> Time: 20 mins | Serves 2
> Net carbs: 8g | Fat: 22g
> Protein: 9g | Kcal: 225

INGREDIENTS

- 2 eggs
- 125ml whole milk
- 2 tbsp butter, melted
- 1 tsp almond extract
- 150g almond flour
- 2 tbsp granulated sweetener
- 1 tsp baking powder
- 1/8 tsp salt
- 30g fresh or frozen raspberries

INSTRUCTIONS

1 Preheat your air fryer to 200 degrees Celsius and line a 7 inch (18 cm) round baking pan with parchment paper.

2 Place the eggs, milk, butter and almond extract in a blender and puree for about thirty seconds.

3 Add the remaining ingredients to the blender and puree until smooth.

4 Pour the pancake batter into the prepared pan and stir in the raspberries gently.

5 Place in the air fryer.

6 Cook for 9 minutes or until the pancake is puffed and the top is golden brown.

7 Slice and serve.

NUTTY GRANOLA

Time: 30 mins | Serves 12
Net carbs: 2g | Fat: 26g
Protein: 7g | Kcal: 278

INGREDIENTS

- 130g almonds, chopped finely
- 50g walnuts, chopped finely
- 50g hazelnuts, peeled, chopped finely
- 115g pecans, chopped finely
- 40g pumpkin seeds
- 40g hemp seeds
- 150g ground flaxseeds
- 1 tsp vanilla
- 1 egg white, whisked
- 60g butter, melted

INSTRUCTIONS

1. Preheat your air fryer to 160 degrees Celsius.
2. Line your air fryer basket with parchment.
3. Place the chopped nuts in a large bowl and then add the pumpkin seeds, hemp seeds and flaxseed. Toss well.
4. Add the remaining ingredients and toss well.
5. Pour the nut mix into the air fryer basket and bake for 18 minutes, tossing halfway through to bake evenly.
6. Empty the granola onto a tray and let cool completely.
7. Serve on its own or with milk.

BACON AND EGG STUFFED PEPPERS

Time: 20 mins | Serves 2
Net carbs: 4g | Fat: 19g
Protein: 14g | Kcal: 148

INGREDIENTS

- 4 eggs
- 2 tbsp heavy cream
- 2 tbsp chopped cooked bacon
- 2 tbsp grated cheddar cheese
- ½ tsp salt
- 1/8 tsp ground black pepper
- 1 large red pepper, cut in half vertically, seeds removed

INSTRUCTIONS

1. Preheat your air fryer to 160 degrees Celsius.
2. Place red pepper halves in the air fryer basket and cook for 5 minutes.
3. In a small bowl, whisk together all the ingredients.
4. Pour the eggs into the partially cooked peppers and bake for 7 minutes.
5. Serve straight out of the baking cup.

VEGETABLE HASH

> Time: 35 mins | Serves 4
> Net carbs: 3g | Fat: 12g
> Protein: 12g | Kcal: 238

INGREDIENTS

- 6 slices bacon, chopped, cooked
- 25g chopped white onion
- 160g Brussel sprouts, sliced in quarters
- 300g diced green bell peppers
- ½ tsp salt
- ½ tsp ground black pepper
- 2 cloves garlic, minced
- 4 eggs, whisked

INSTRUCTIONS

1. Preheat your air fryer to 180 degrees Celsius.
2. Toss the bacon, onion, Brussel sprouts, bell peppers, salt, pepper and garlic together in a large bowl.
3. Pour the mix into a 7 inch (18 cm) pan that will fit in your air fryer basket.
4. Place in the air fryer and cook for 15 minutes.
5. Pour the whisked eggs in the basket and return the pan to the air fryer to cook for 10 more minutes.
6. Mix well to break up the hash and serve while hot.

HAM, CHEESE AND MUSHROOM MELT

> Time: 30 mins | Serves 4
> Net carbs: 4g | Fat: 22g
> Protein: 34g | Kcal: 352

INGREDIENTS

- 2 tbsp butter
- 250g sliced mushrooms
- 1 clove garlic, minced
- 35g white onion, diced
- 30-450g ham steak, cooked
- 55g cooked, crumbled bacon
- 1 tbsp fresh parsley, chopped
- 235g grated cheddar cheese

INSTRUCTIONS

1 Preheat your air fryer to 180 degrees Celsius.

2 In a pan that will fit inside your air fryer, combine the butter and diced onion.

3 Place in the preheated air fryer and cook for 5 minutes.

4 Remove the pan from the air fryer and stir in the garlic and mushrooms.

5 Return to the air fryer for another 5 minutes.

6 Remove the pan again and add the ham steak, pushing it toward the bottom of the pan.

7 Top with the bacon and grated cheese and place in the air fryer for another 8 minutes.

8 Move the ham steak and pan contents to a plate, garnish with the parsley and serve while hot.

SIDES

EASY CHIPS

Time: 30 mins | Serves 4
Net carbs: 2g | Fat: 4g
Protein: 1g | Kcal: 40

INGREDIENTS

- 2 medium-large potatoes
- 1 tbsp olive oil
- 1 tsp salt
- ½ tsp ground black pepper

INSTRUCTIONS

1. Preheat your air fryer to 200 degrees Celsius.
2. Slice the potatoes into 8mm strips, choosing to peel them or not.
3. Toss the potatoes in a medium-sized bowl with olive oil and seasoning.
4. Place the potatoes on the air fryer tray or in the air fryer basket.
5. Cook for 20 mins, tossing the potatoes occasionally to allow them to cook evenly.
6. Once crisp and golden, remove the chips from the air fryer and serve.

SPICY HOT PEPPER NACHOS

Time: 20 mins | Serves 6
Net carbs: 5g | Fat: 22g
Protein: 7g | Kcal: 377

INGREDIENTS

- 1 tbsp chili powder
- 1 tsp ground cumin
- 1 tsp salt
- ½ tsp ground black pepper
- 1 tsp garlic powder
- ½ tsp fresh chopped cilantro
- 500g ground turkey
- 500g red bell peppers, cut into strips
- 1 jalapeno, sliced
- 1 tsp sriracha sauce
- 340g grated cheddar cheese

INSTRUCTIONS

1 Preheat your air fryer to 200 degrees Celsius.
2 Mix the spices in a small bowl.
3 Add the turkey to a large skillet and cook until browned. Stir in the spice mix.
4 Place the bell pepper strips in a lightly greased baking pan and top with the cooked turkey, jalapeno and cheese.
5 Place the pan in the air fryer and cook for 8 minutes to melt and lightly brown the cheese.
6 Drizzle sriracha over the top and serve while hot.

CRANBERRY DARK CHOCOLATE GRANOLA BARS

> Time: 35 mins | Serves 16
> Net carbs: 3g | Fat: 16g
> Protein: 3g | Kcal: 179

INGREDIENTS

- 230g unsweetened shredded coconut
- 130g sliced almonds
- 75g chopped pecans
- 45g dried cranberries
- 55g unsweetened, dark chocolate chips
- 85g hemp seeds
- ½ tsp salt
- 115g butter
- 2 tsp keto maple syrup
- 25g powdered sweetener
- ½ tsp vanilla

INSTRUCTIONS

1 Preheat your air fryer to 150 degrees Celsius and line the air fryer tray with parchment paper.

2 Add the coconut, nuts and hemp seeds to a food processor and pulse until well mixed and crumbly.

3 Place the mix in a large bowl along with the cranberries, dark chocolate chips and salt.

4 In a small pot, melt the butter and maple syrup over low heat.

5 Whisk in the sweetener and stir until melted. Turn off the heat and add the vanilla extract.

6 Pour the butter mix over the nut mix and stir quickly to coat evenly.

7   Pour the mix onto the prepared sheet tray and press down so the mix is compact and even.

8   Place the tray in the oven and bake for 20 minutes, until the edges turn slightly brown.

9   Cool the bars completely and then slice and serve.

HERBY CHEESY MUFFINS

> Time: 45 mins | Serves 12
> Net carbs: 4g | Fat: 27g
> Protein: 13g | Kcal: 322

INGREDIENTS

- 6 tbsp melted butter
- 35g minced garlic
- 120g sour cream
- 4 eggs
- 240g almond flour
- 125g coconut flour
- 2 tsp baking powder
- 235g shredded cheddar cheese
- 8g chopped parsley
- ½ tsp dried basil
- ½ tsp dried, chopped rosemary

INSTRUCTIONS

1. Preheat your air fryer to 160 degrees Celsius and spray a muffin tin or individual muffin cups with cooking spray.
2. Place the sour cream, 1 tbsp garlic, eggs and salt in a food processor and puree until smooth.
3. Add the flours, cheddar cheese, and herbs to the food processor and pulse until a smooth dough forms.
4. Scoop the batter into the muffin cups.
5. Combine the melted butter and the remaining garlic and then brush the tops of each muffin with the butter mix.
6. Place the muffins in the air fryer and bake for 25 minutes or until the tops are golden brown.
7. Cool before serving.

CHEDDAR CRACKERS

Time: 1 hour | Serves 10
Net carbs: 2g | Fat: 18g
Protein: 9g | Kcal: 218

INGREDIENTS

- 200g sunflower seeds
- 170g cheddar cheese, grated
- 2 tbsp Italian seasoning
- 80g chia seeds
- ½ tsp garlic powder
- ½ tsp baking powder
- 1 egg
- 2 tbsp butter, melted
- Salt

INSTRUCTIONS

1 Preheat your air fryer to 150 degrees Celsius.
2 Place the sunflower seeds and chia seeds in a food processor until finely blended into a powder. Place in a large bowl.
3 Add the cheese, Italian seasoning, garlic powder and baking powder to the bowl and mix well.
4 Add in the melted butter and egg and stir until a nice dough forms.
5 Place the dough on a piece of parchment and then place another piece of parchment on top.
6 Roll the dough into a thin sheet about 1/8 inch thick.
7 Remove the top piece of parchment and lift the dough using the bottom parchment and place on a sheet tray that will fit in the air fryer.

8 Score the cracker dough into your desired shape and then bake for 40-45 minutes.

9 Break the crackers apart and serve.

CAULIFLOWER CRUNCH

Time: 6 hours | Serves 4
Net carbs: 3g | Fat: 3g
Protein: 1g | Kcal: 55

INGREDIENTS

- 280g cauliflower florets, chopped into bite-sized pieces
- 1 tbsp olive oil
- 1 tsp sea salt

INSTRUCTIONS

1. Preheat your air fryer to 60 degrees Celsius.
2. Wash and drain the cauliflower florets.
3. Place the cauliflower in a large bowl and toss with the olive oil and sea salt.
4. Add the cauliflower to the basket of your air fryer or spread them in a flat layer on the tray of your air fryer (either option will work!).
5. Cook in the air fryer for about 6 hours, tossing the cauliflower every hour or so to dehydrate evenly.
6. Once the cauliflower is fully dried, remove it from the air fryer and then let cool.
7. Enjoy fresh or store in an airtight container for up to a month.

CHILI LIME BROCCOLI CRUNCH

> Time: 6 hours | Serves 4
> Net carbs: 1g | Fat: 3g
> Protein: 2g | Kcal: 62

INGREDIENTS

- 280g broccoli florets, chopped into bite-sized pieces
- 1 tbsp olive oil
- 1 tsp sea salt
- 1 tsp lime zest
- 1 tbsp lime juice
- 1 tsp chili powder

INSTRUCTIONS

1. Preheat your air fryer to 60 degrees Celsius.
2. Wash and drain the broccoli florets.
3. Place the broccoli in a large bowl and toss with the olive oil, lime juice, lime zest and sea salt.
4. Add the broccoli to the basket of your air fryer or spread them in a flat layer on the tray of your air fryer.
5. Cook in the air fryer for about 6 hours, tossing the broccoli every hour or so to dehydrate evenly.
6. Once the broccoli is fully dried, remove it from the air fryer, toss with the chili powder, and then let it cool.
7. Enjoy fresh or store in an airtight container for up to a month.

ZUCCHINI CHIPS

Time: 4 hours | Serves 8
Net carbs: 2g | Fat: 4g
Protein: 1g | Kcal: 40

INGREDIENTS

- 120g very thin zucchini slices
- 2 tbsp olive oil
- 2 tsp sea salt

INSTRUCTIONS

1 Preheat your air fryer to 60 degrees Celsius.
2 Toss the thin zucchini slices with the oil and sea salt.
3 Place the zucchini on the air fryer tray or in the air fryer basket.
4 Cook for 4 hours, tossing the zucchini occasionally to allow it to dehydrate evenly.
5 Once crisp, remove the zucchini from the air fryer and serve.

SEA SALT AND BLACK PEPPER CUCUMBER CHIPS

Time: 3 hours | Serves 4
Net carbs: 3g | Fat: 0g
Protein: 1g | Kcal: 16

INGREDIENTS

- 120g very thin cucumber slices
- 2 tbsp apple cider vinegar
- 2 tsp sea salt
- 1 tsp ground black pepper

INSTRUCTIONS

1 Preheat your air fryer to 100 degrees Celsius.
2 Place the cucumber slices on a paper towel and layer another paper towel on top to absorb the moisture in the cucumbers.
3 Place the dried slices in a large bowl and toss with the vinegar, ground black pepper, and salt.
4 Place the cucumber slices on a tray lined with parchment and then bake in the air fryer for 3 hours. The cucumbers will begin to curl and brown slightly.
5 Turn off the air fryer and let the cucumber slices cool inside the fryer.
6 Serve right away or store in an airtight container.

SOFT CINNAMON PRETZELS

Time: 30 mins | Serves 6
Net carbs: 6g | Fat: 34g
Protein: 28g | Kcal: 432

INGREDIENTS

- 240g almond flour
- 1 tbsp baking powder
- 1 tsp salt
- 3 eggs
- 5 tbsp softened cream cheese
- 500g mozzarella cheese, grated
- ½ tsp ground cinnamon

INSTRUCTIONS

1. Preheat your air fryer to 200 degrees Celsius and prepare the air fryer tray with parchment paper.
2. Place the almond flour, baking powder and salt in a large bowl and stir well.
3. Combine the cream cheese and mozzarella in a separate bowl and melt in the microwave, heating slowly and stirring several times to ensure the cheese melts and does not burn.
4. Add two eggs to the almond flour mix along with the melted cheese. Stir well until a dough forms.
5. Divide the dough into six equal pieces and roll into your desired pretzel shape.
6. Place the pretzels on the prepared sheet tray.
7. Whisk the remaining eggs and brush over the pretzels then sprinkle them all with the cinnamon.

8   Bake in the air fryer for 12 minutes or until the pretzels are golden brown.

9   Remove from the air fryer and serve while warm.

SWEET CANDIED PECANS

Time: 15 mins | Serves 6
Net carbs: 7g | Fat: 34g
Protein: 14g | Kcal: 409

INGREDIENTS

- 1 egg white
- 330g whole pecans
- 2 tsp salt
- 1 tbsp sweetener

INSTRUCTIONS

1 Preheat your air fryer to 160 degrees Celsius and prepare the air fryer tray with parchment paper.
2 Place the egg whites in a large bowl and whip until stiff peaks form.
3 Add the almonds and toss to coat.
4 Sprinkle with the sweetener and salt and then place the almonds on the tray, laying them out as evenly as possible on the tray.
5 Bake in the air fryer for 10 minutes. The almonds should be golden brown.
6 Remove from the air fryer and let cool before serving.

DESSERTS

CHOCOLATE CHIP COOKIES

> Time: 20 mins | Serves 12
> Net carbs: 1g | Fat: 18g
> Protein: 4g | Kcal: 168

INGREDIENTS

- 115g butter, melted
- 40g sweetener
- 1 tsp vanilla extract
- 1 egg
- 190g almond flour
- 1/2 tsp salt
- 1/2 tsp baking powder
- 120g sugar-free chocolate chips

INSTRUCTIONS

1 Preheat your air fryer to 170 degrees Celsius and prepare your air fryer tray with a piece of parchment.

2 Beat the melted butter and sweetener together in a large bowl.

3 Add the eggs and vanilla and mix until the batter comes together.

4 Add the salt, baking powder and almond flour and mix until a nice, smooth batter forms.

5 Fold in the chocolate chips then add 12 scoops of the cookie dough onto the prepared sheet tray, leaving 5 cm between each one.

6 Bake the cookies in the air fryer for 8-9 minutes or until golden brown on the edges.

7 Let cool on the sheet tray for 5 minutes before removing and serving.

PEANUT BUTTER CHOCOLATE CHIP COOKIES

INGREDIENTS

- 120g peanut butter
- 25g sweetener
- 1 egg yolk
- 1/2 tsp vanilla extract
- 1/8 tsp sea salt
- 40g dark chocolate chips

INSTRUCTIONS

1. Preheat your air fryer to 110 degrees Celsius and prepare the air fryer tray with parchment paper.
2. Combine all the ingredients in a large bowl and mix until a dough forms.
3. Add 5 scoops of the dough onto the sheet tray and use a fork to flatten them, adding peanut butter on the top.
4. Bake in the air fryer for 12 minutes.
5. Allow to cool before removing from the tray and serving.

PUMPKIN SPICE COOKIES

> Time: 20 mins | Serves 12
> Net carbs: 3g | Fat: 16g
> Protein: 4g | Kcal: 188

INGREDIENTS

- 60g butter, melted
- 50ml pumpkin puree
- 25g sweetener
- 1 tsp vanilla extract
- 1 egg
- 125g almond flour
- 1/2 tsp salt
- 1 tsp pumpkin spice seasoning
- 1/2 tsp baking powder

INSTRUCTIONS

1. Preheat your air fryer to 160 degrees Celsius and prepare your air fryer tray with a piece of parchment.
2. Beat the melted butter, pumpkin puree and sweetener together in a large bowl.
3. Add the eggs and vanilla and mix until the batter forms.
4. Add the salt, baking powder, pumpkin spice seasoning and almond flour and mix until a smooth batter forms.
5. Add 12 scoops of cookie dough onto the sheet tray, leaving 5 cm between each one.
6. Bake the cookies in the air fryer for 8-9 minutes or until golden brown on the edges.
7. Cool on the sheet tray for 5 minutes before removing and serving.

CHOCOLATE CAKE

> Time: 1 hour | Serves 12
> Net carbs: 4g | Fat: 36g
> Protein: 11g | Kcal: 348

INGREDIENTS

- 315g almond flour
- 35g coconut flour
- 40g chocolate protein powder
- 1/2 tsp salt
- 30g unsweetened cocoa powder
- 1 tbsp baking powder
- 160g granulated sweetener
- 115g butter
- 175ml whole milk
- 1 tsp vanilla
- 4 whole eggs

INSTRUCTIONS

1 Preheat your air fryer to 160 degrees Celsius and grease an 8 inch (20 cm) cake pan.

2 Place the butter in a mixing bowl along with the sweetener and beat until fluffy.

3 In a separate bowl for wet ingredients, mix the eggs, milk and vanilla.

4 In a third bowl for dry ingredients, combine the almond flour, coconut flour, chocolate protein powder, salt, cocoa powder, and baking powder.

5 Add half of the wet mixture to the bowl with the fluffy butter and beat together slowly.

6 Add half of the dry mix to the bowl and beat again until smooth.

7   Add the remaining wet ingredients, mix and add the remaining dry ingredients and blend until a smooth batter forms.

8   Pour the cake batter into the prepared pan and place in the air fryer to cook for 30 minutes, until golden brown and a toothpick comes out cleanly when inserted into the centre of the cake.

9   Remove from the air fryer and cool in the pan for 20 minutes.

10 Flip the cake out of the pan, slice and serve.

VANILLA RASPBERRY CAKE

Time: 1 hour | Serves 12
Net carbs: 10g | Fat: 32g
Protein: 10g | Kcal: 368

INGREDIENTS

- 315g almond flour
- 30g coconut flour
- 40g vanilla protein powder
- 1/2 tsp salt
- 1 tbsp baking powder
- 25g granulated sweetener
- 115g butter
- 175ml whole milk
- 1 tsp vanilla
- 4 whole eggs
- 170g fresh raspberries

INSTRUCTIONS

1. Preheat your air fryer to 160 degrees Celsius and grease an 8 inch (20 cm) cake pan.
2. Place the butter in a mixing bowl along with the sweetener and beat until fluffy.
3. In a separate bowl for wet ingredients, mix the eggs, milk and vanilla.
4. In a third bowl for dry ingredients, combine the remaining almond flour, coconut flour, vanilla protein powder, salt, cocoa powder, and baking powder.
5. Add half of the wet mixture to the bowl with the fluffy butter and beat together slowly.
6. Add half of the dry mix to the bowl and beat again until smooth.

7   Add the remaining wet ingredients, mix and add the remaining dry ingredients and blend until a smooth batter forms.

8   Gently stir in the raspberries.

9   Pour the cake batter into the prepared pan and place in the air fryer to cook for 30 minutes, until golden brown and a toothpick comes out cleanly when inserted into the centre of the cake.

10 Remove from the air fryer and cool in the pan for 20 minutes.

11 Flip the cake out of the pan, slice and serve.

STRAWBERRY CHEESECAKE

Time: 1 ½ hours | Serves 12
Net carbs: 6g | Fat: 26g
Protein: 5g | Kcal: 315

INGREDIENTS

- 750g cream cheese
- 5 tbsp butter
- 25g powdered sweetener
- 3 eggs
- 1 ½ tsp vanilla extract
- 185g sour cream
- 125g chopped, fresh strawberries

INSTRUCTIONS

1. Preheat your air fryer to 140 degrees Celsius, grease an 8 inch (20 cm) springform cake pan, and add a piece of parchment in the bottom of the pan.
2. Place the cream cheese and butter in a large bowl and beat until combined.
3. Add the powdered sweetener and beat again until smooth.
4. Add the eggs, one at a time, allowing them to fully mix in after adding each one.
5. Add the sour cream and vanilla extract and stir one last time, until the batter is smooth and all the ingredients are well blended.
6. Fold in the chopped strawberries.
7. Pour the batter into the prepared cake pan and then place the pan on a larger tray with high sides that will fit in the air fryer.
8. Fill the pan with water, creating a water bath for the cheesecake.

9   Place in the preheated air fryer and bake for an hour and 15 minutes.

10 Allow the cheesecake to cool for 3 hours in the fridge before removing from the pan and serving.

LEMON CHEESECAKE

Time: 1 ½ hours | Serves 12
Net carbs: 1g | Fat: 27g
Protein: 5g | Kcal: 294

INGREDIENTS

- 750g cream cheese
- 5 tbsp butter
- 25g powdered sweetener
- 3 eggs
- 1 ½ tsp vanilla extract
- 185g sour cream
- 1 tsp lemon zest

INSTRUCTIONS

1. Preheat your air fryer to 140 degrees Celsius, grease an 8 inch (20 cm) springform cake pan, and add a piece of parchment in the bottom of the pan.
2. Place the cream cheese and butter in a large bowl and beat until combined.
3. Add the powdered sweetener and beat again until smooth.
4. Add the eggs, one at a time, allowing them to fully mix in after each addition.
5. Add the sour cream, lemon zest and vanilla extract and stir one last time, making sure the batter is smooth and all the ingredients are well blended.
6. Pour the batter into the prepared cake pan and then place the pan on a larger tray with high sides that will fit in the air fryer.
7. Fill the pan with water, creating a water bath for the cheesecake.

8 Place in the preheated air fryer and bake for an hour and 15 minutes.

9 Allow the cheesecake to cool for 3 hours in the fridge before removing from the pan and serving.

FUDGE BROWNIES

Time: 35 mins | Serves 16
Net carbs: 1g | Fat: 4g
Protein: 3g | Kcal: 110

INGREDIENTS

- 115g melted butter
- 15g sweetener
- 1/2 tsp vanilla extract
- 3 room temperature eggs
- 65g almond flour
- 40g unsweetened cocoa powder
- 1 tbsp plain, unsweetened gelatin
- 1/2 tsp salt
- 1/2 tsp baking powder
- 50ml water

INSTRUCTIONS

1 Preheat your air fryer to 160 degrees Celsius and grease an 8x8 inch (20x20 cm) square baking pan.
2 Combine the eggs, vanilla extract, swerve, and melted butter in a bowl and whisk together well.
3 Add the cocoa powder, almond flour, baking powder, gelatin, and salt and whisk again until smooth.
4 Add the water and stir again.
5 Pour the batter into the greased baking pan and place in the pre-heated air fryer.

6   Bake for 15 minutes, until the centre is a little wet and the edges are firmer.

7   Let the brownies cool in the pan before slicing and serving.

CHOCOLATE MINT BROWNIES

Time: 35 mins | Serves 16
Net carbs: 1g | Fat: 4g
Protein: 3g | Kcal: 110

INGREDIENTS

- 115g melted butter
- 15g sweetener
- 1⁄2 tsp peppermint extract
- 3 room temperature eggs
- 65g almond flour
- 40g unsweetened cocoa powder
- 1 tbsp plain, unsweetened gelatin
- 1⁄2 tsp salt
- 1⁄2 tsp baking powder
- 50ml water

INSTRUCTIONS

1 Preheat your air fryer to 160 degrees Celsius and grease an 8x8 inch (20x20 cm) square baking pan.
2 Combine the eggs, peppermint extract, swerve, and melted butter in a bowl and whisk together well.
3 Add the cocoa powder, almond flour, baking powder, gelatin, and salt and whisk again until smooth.
4 Add the water and stir again.
5 Pour the batter into the greased baking pan and place in the preheated air fryer.

6 Bake for 15 minutes, until the centre is a little wet and the edges are firmer.

7 Let the brownies cool in the pan before slicing and serving.

KETO SHORTBREAD

Time: 30 mins | Serves 8
Net carbs: 2g | Fat: 18g
Protein: 3g | Kcal: 18

INGREDIENTS

- 115g butter
- 12g swerve sweetener
- 1 tsp vanilla extract
- 125g almond flour
- 1 tsp salt

INSTRUCTIONS

1   Preheat your air fryer to 150 degrees Celsius and grease a 6 inch (15 cm) baking pan or tray.
2   Place the butter and sweetener into a mixing bowl and beat until soft and fluffy.
3   Add the vanilla extract and beat again to incorporate fully.
4   Add the almond flour slowly, mixing it in a little at a time, until a smooth dough has formed.
5   Spread the shortbread batter in the prepared baking pan or tray and then place in the preheated air fryer.
6   Bake for 15 minutes or until the edges of the shortbread are golden brown.
7   Let cool for 10 minutes then flip the shortbread out of the pan, slice and serve while warm.

BONUS: 30-Day Air Fryer Meal Plan

Menu

Spicy Fried Chicken
Chicken Patties
Classic Meatballs
Salmon and Asparagus
Lemon Pepper Fish Sticks
Spicy Egg Salad
Three Cheese Omelette

Shopping List

900g chicken breast
145g pork skin
500g minced beef
880g salmon fillets
500g cod
Asparagus spears
Parsley
Whole milk

Whey protein powder
Grated parmesan
Mozzarella
Cheddar cheese
Eggs
Almond flour
Lemon pepper seasoning
Heavy whipping cream

Already have?

Lemon juice
Mayonnaise
Mustard
Olive oil
Apple cider vinegar
Italian seasoning
Paprika
Cayenne Pepper
Salt
Ground black pepper

Days 8 - 14

Menu

BBQ Fried Chicken
Prosciutto Wrapped Chicken
Italian Lasagna
Dijon Baked Salmon
Lemon Dill Wrapped Cod
Roasted Veggie Soup
Coconut Chocolate Pancake

Shopping List

1kg chicken breast	Whole milk
240g minced beef	Heavy cream
750g salmon	Butter
500g cod fillets	Whey protein powder
Prosciutto de parma	Grated parmesan
Vegetable broth	Ricotta
Baby spinach	Mozzarella
Parsley	Eggs
Dill	Olive oil
Thyme	BBQ sauce
Cauliflower	Marinara sauce
broccoli	Coconut flour
Zucchini	Cocoa powder
Green bell pepper	Sweetener
Carrot	Shredded coconut

Already have?

Vanilla extract	Italian seasoning
Olive oil	Salt
Lemon juice	Ground black pepper
Garlic	
Baking powder	
Paprika	

Days 15 - 21

Menu

Rotisserie-Style Chicken Thighs
Chicken Patties
Creamy Garlic Pork Chops
Red Hot Tuna Cakes
Crab Stuffed Mushrooms
Pumpkin Soup
Spinach Parmesan Baked Egg

Shopping List

500g chicken thighs	Onion
400g chicken breast	Pumpkin
215g pork skin	Mushrooms
500g pork chops	Mozzarella
340g fresh crab meat	Soft cheese
Eggs	Cheddar cheese
Chicken broth	Parmesan
Canned tuna	Sour cream
Asparagus	Lemon
Zucchini	Heavy cream
Carrots	Red pepper flakes
Spinach	

Already have?

Olive oil	Mayonnaise
Mustard	Paprika
Lemon juice	Sea salt
Garlic	Ground black pepper
Oregano	
Thyme	

Days 22 - 30

Menu

Lemon Garlic Chicken Thighs
Fajita Chicken
Buffalo Chicken Pizza
Minty Lamb Chops
Tuna Sticks
Garlic Butter Shrimp
Spinach and Sundried Tomato Casserole
Bacon and Egg Stuffed Peppers
Vegetable Hash

Shopping List

500g chicken thighs
1kg chicken breast
500g lamb chops
45g pork skin
500g tuna
500g shrimp
Bacon
Vegetable stock
Lemon
Green bell peppers
Zucchini
Brussel sprouts
Baby spinach
Sundried tomatoes
Onion

Red pepper
Mint
Fajita seasoning
Parmesan
Mozzarella
Cheddar cheese
Parmesan
Ricotta
Eggs
Almond flour
Buffalo sauce
Whole milk
Butter
Heavy cream

Already have?

Olive oil
Mayonnaise
Mustard
Basil

Parsley
Thyme
Garlic
Lemon juice

Sea salt
Ground black pepper

DISCLAIMER

This book contains opinions and ideas of the author and is meant to teach the reader informative and helpful knowledge while due care should be taken by the user in the application of the information provided. The instructions and strategies are possibly not right for every reader and there is no guarantee that they work for everyone. Using this book and implementing the information/recipes therein contained is explicitly your own responsibility and risk. This work with all its contents, does not guarantee correctness, completion, quality or correctness of the provided information. Misinformation or misprints cannot be completely eliminated.

Printed in Great Britain
by Amazon